WINTER MOON

WINTER MOON

A Season of Zen Teachings

Bonnie Myotai Treace

HERMITAGE HEART PUBLICATIONS

An Alice Peck Editorial Book

ISBN 978-0-9860587-7-6
First Edition, December 2013
Book design by Duane Stapp

Dedication

To my mom, who always knew, and it was love.
And to my teachers, who said not to know,
And that, too, was quite likely love.

Contents

Prologue

The Snow Man

One must have a mind of winter
To regard the frost and the boughs
Of the pine-trees crusted with snow;

And have been cold a long time
To behold the junipers shagged with ice,
The spruces rough in the distant glitter

Of the January sun; and not to think
Of any misery in the sound of the wind,
In the sound of a few leaves,

Which is the sound of the land
Full of the same wind
That is blowing in the same bare place

For the listener, who listens in the snow,
And, nothing himself, beholds
Nothing that is not there and the nothing that is.

—Wallace Stevens

A specific moment after a January snowstorm. As specific as any moment, any life. A specific perspective, and with it, all the implicit questions, poignant matters, and beautiful possibilities of this life. Some would say Zen is "about" what happens when we stop adding on, decorating, dragging along our baggage moment by moment—when, as Stevens says, we've been "cold a long time." The night moon through bare trees; no one looking for anything else, nothing better. The wind is just the wind, and there is no counting of minutes, no watching of the clock. The thing is, as "The Snow Man" so adeptly and subtly presents, the shadowed snow will reflect the mind's persistent patterns of seeing. No matter how much one sets down, there it is, rather emotively calling the junipers "shagged," the pines "crusted," the spruces "rough." We still know something, even if it's that we know we don't know, and in a hair's breadth, knower and known are separate, and the dualities align in their familiar places.

Is there an intimate and authentic life? The leaf barely moving, the imperceptible breeze: the snowman beholds everything everywhere "full of the same wind…blowing in the same bare place." The place of that place is the matter at hand. To point anywhere else is to miss it. Yet to point here is also to miss it. Not to point is also to miss it. Yet the question is at the heart of our lives. Are we called in this to "do something" in order to awaken, break free from the ruts and self-delusions that hold us in trance, and bind us from making a generous and maybe joyful offering to all beings? Doing nothing isn't sufficient. Doing something is inadequate. In Zen we call this the red-hot iron ball that can't quite be swallowed, and can't quite be spit out: it is the *koan* of being. This is, in a way, all that we study in the talks that comprise *Winter Moon*.

"For the listener, who listens in the snow"... snow is hearing snow. There is no stranger here. Though the practice of Zen is on the one hand essentially uncomfortable (yes, there is that hot-iron-ball-in-the-throat image), it is also a process of coming home to an honest and honorable way of life. In this sense, the moon is in the room—and we are specifically, one might even say perfectly, capable of this.

The pieces in this book were first written over a ten-year period, and presented as dharma discourses at Zen Mountain Monastery and Fire Lotus Temple, where I studied and taught in the Mountains and Rivers Order (MRO). As the first dharma successor of John Daido Loori Roshi, I served as Vice-Abbot of the Monastery and establishing Abbot of the Temple. At the time, I was living as a monastic, and several of the talks in *Winter Moon* use formal koans as the basis of their presentation. Koan study, part of the training of many MRO Zen students, developed separately in the two great Buddhist traditions that became Rinzai and Soto Zen. Rinzai teachers tended to organize koans into a kind of curriculum, while Soto teachers tended to select koans for each particular student. The Soto monk Harada Sogaku broke from this tradition, studied with Rinzai masters, and created a way of drawing from the wisdom of both. He and another Soto teacher created what became known as the Harada-Yasutani school, which formed a background for the way Daido Roshi and his teacher Maezumi Roshi eventually taught their students. I was very fortunate in being able to study with both of them over a course of nearly thirty years, and since the basic vow is that Zen training is never over, I'm pretty sure that though "gone from this life," they're not finished with me yet. Just as love is never finished, and the edge of the self cannot be found. May their dharma continue to kick up trouble wherever we settle in.

Hermitage Heart

A scent of wood smoke and incense, wind wrapping itself around a small hut, the quiet presence of a settled, generous spiritual friend: to sit with the poems of the nineteenth-century Buddhist nun Rengetsu is to allow a teacher into the depths of one's mind. Over the winter, this is often my practice, taking up a few of Rengetsu's winter-inspired *waka* verses (short poems) from the John Stevens translation, *Lotus Moon,* and staying with them, committing myself to let them inform whatever teaching happens during this time.

Keeping that commitment hasn't always been easy. Some of Rengetsu's writing is so strong that it is immediately engaging, and stirs the sense of trust and humility that comes so naturally when excellence takes hold of one's attention. Nothing truer or finer beckons; restlessness slips away. But some of her verses, like many of the classic koans in the collections used in Zen training, lie a little flat initially and take more work to open up. Since commitment to any practice means not moving to something easier when it gets difficult, the challenge has been to stay with the words and give even her harder-to-appreciate poems time to work on the heart and soften the impulse to reject them and move on.

Rengetsu lived what could have easily become a tragic life. She was born the daughter of a courtesan and a samurai, but her natural father had her adopted by a lay priest serving at Chionji, Japan's head temple of the Pure Land sect of Buddhism. Rengetsu's adoptive father, Teruhisa, seems to have been devoted to her. He taught her martial arts, calligraphy, and an appreciation for art and literature, which later—in a certain way—would save her life. For several years she served as an attendant to the lord of Kameoka, a city near Kyoto, and was fortunate in being able to continue her classical education while there. Stevens writes, charmingly, that "Rengetsu was just as capable of disarming intruders and subduing annoying drunks as she was at making poetry and performing the tea ceremony."

But then the challenges began to roll in: she was married off, had three children who died in early infancy, and separated from a husband who abused her, and who also died shortly thereafter. She married again, and while she was pregnant with their second child, her husband became ill and passed away. Try to imagine, if you will, this woman's life: thirty-three years old, with two small children, having experienced more heartbreak and loss than most of us will know in a lifetime. If ever there was an excuse for feeling overwhelmed and depressed, her life certainly offered one.

One pleasure of discovering the lives and teachings of the rare women we find in the history of Buddhism is seeing how they take up the tragedies in their lives and transform them. They remind us of the freedom that no circumstances can steal from us. Because their stories are generally less accessible—and because the luxury of serious religious training was less available to them—finding someone like Rengetsu is a great gift. She faced this moment in her life when despair could have taken hold, when impermanence had pretty much whipped her to the bone, and somehow her heart sparked. She became ordained as a nun, taking her children with her to live on the grounds of Chionji with Teruhisa, and practiced in earnest. Still, death kept coming, and by the time she was forty-one, her remaining children and the adoptive father she had loved since childhood were gone. Not allowed to remain at Chionji, she then had to find her way alone.

She walked into a world that attempted to limit her on the basis of her gender. It's said she considered whether she could make a living as a teacher of the game of Go, at which she excelled, but she recognized that few male students would be able to muster student-mind with a female teacher. She soon realized that art would be her path, and began making pottery as a kind of moving meditation, inscribing each piece with a bit of poetry.

Over time her work became immensely popular, so much so that she found it necessary to never stay long in any one place, or crowds would begin to gather around her. Likening herself to a "drifting cloud," she was still prolific, with her work becoming one of the most generous, sustained offerings of deep spiritual practice in Buddhist history. Reputedly, she was able to raise large sums of money for disaster victims because of her ability to be as at ease intermingling with the statesmen and great artists of her day as she was meditating or making pottery alone in her hut. When she died in 1875 at the age of eighty-four, she left a legacy of more than fifty thousand pieces of pottery, calligraphy, paintings, and poetry. She is remembered not as a tragic figure, but as one of those rare human beings who drew from a seemingly bottomless well of strength and love.

The three Rengetsu winter poems that I'm especially fond of have a straightforward, unadorned quality, as does most of her writing. And although she did not organize them into the sequence in which they appear in Stevens's book, their progression struck me as—however inadvertently—expressing a spiritual journey itself.

I advised a friend of mine who was stymied on a writing project to try the device that novelists sometimes use to provide a frame for their stories: "Chapter One—in which a man goes in search of a whale." Then I decided to give my own advice a try: "Three Poems of Rengetsu—in which a spiritual journey is indicated, though never baldly named...in which what is subtle and intuitive is immediate and uncomplicated... in which what is interior and private is also the exterior condition, the public expression." So I took *Lotus Moon: The Poetry of the Buddhist Nun Rengetsu,* translated by John Stevens, down from the shelf and ended up making what wasn't a sequence of poems into a journey. It began with:

Winter Confinement in Shigaraki Village

Last night's storm was fierce
As I can see by this morning's
Thick blanket of snow:
Rising to kindle woodchips,
In lonely Shigaraki Village.

Shigaraki Village is where Rengetsu would go to get the clay for her pottery. This is such a beautifully simple poem. A woman enters a hut, she's traveled some distance, she's worked all day. Darkness comes. At dawn, she sees snow blanketing the hills and knows that there must have been a fierce storm in the night. She kindles the fire. In its thusness, it is just thus.

But as we stay with the poem, we might find ourselves reflecting on the journey we make to find the clay for our own vessel. We might begin to wonder about leaving home and coming to dwell alone. During periods of intensive Zen training, for instance, each of us is asked to leave our familiar patterns and deepen our practice: to dwell peacefully in each moment's sufficiency, making our home there. When monastics ordain, it's the same deal; we become *unsui,* "clouds and water," letting go of the activities in our lives that are self-securing, and giving ourselves to the journey that is itself our home. So, when the poet makes her pilgrimage to Shigaraki, to go with her is to take that journey as well. Will we go, gather the clay for our real work, and settle into the moment?

In Shigaraki Village, the poet is waking up. She's inferring from the evidence the realities of a night's storm. It's interesting that in the Buddhist tradition, night is often used to point to total intimacy, the reality of oneness, of not separating the self from things. In the night, or "darkness," there is no distinction, no separation between seer and seen. In the words of the Heart Sutra, it is the time of "no eye, ear, nose, tongue, body, mind." What is that night? Of course, when many of us begin to sense the "fierce storm" of night in spiritual life, we may yearn for nothing but to be elsewhere. On the edge of it, we pull back, trying to hold onto something of ourselves.

Haven't you felt that resistance that thrives right on the cusp of breaking through? There, on the edge, most of us have some kind of argument. "I can't sit another minute," we say. Or, "I can't see this koan." Or, "I don't know how to love this person." The poem points to a kind of sweet constancy, the kindling of the fire. Just take care of the moment. Stoke the flame when it falters. The poet stirs the wood chips; we stir our lives to find the warm center of things. What is that center?

Zen Master Dogen wrote, "When the dharma does not fill your whole body and mind, you think it is already sufficient. When the dharma fills your body and mind, you understand that something is missing." What is needed? The world has never depended more than it does now on those who will genuinely ask that question. Always encourage one another to go deeply into that inquiry. How might you serve? What remains to be seen?

Dogen continued, "To study the Buddha way is to study the self. To study the self is to forget the self. To forget the self is to be confirmed by the ten thousand things. To be confirmed by the ten thousand things is to cast off body and mind of self as well as that of others. No trace of realization remains, and this no trace is continued endlessly."

The fire of our freedom will always warm the hut, but somehow we won't feel it unless we kindle it. And that kindling of the fire continues. It's not on the clock, like a workday we can't wait to see end. It's loving, and essentially timeless. Practically, getting this point means we're relieved of feeling we're behind or progressing too slowly in our training, or that we're spiritually talented and should set our sights on becoming teachers. It's just time to kindle the woodchips: get over yourself.

In the hut where she's come to make the vessel, responsible for the fire, awake to the night's storm as it was revealed only in the light, the poet then faces the day.

A second poem:

A Day of Hail

Will the paper
On my makeshift
Little window
Withstand the assault
Of the hailstones?

A poem in which a woman, alone in a hut, wonders if her small window made of fragile paper will be strong enough not to be ripped apart by a long day of pelting hail. Simple enough: the sound of heavy stones of solid water hitting and hitting and hitting, the paper window pocking with each strike, quivering, providing such a thin barrier against the storm.

What is this makeshift window—this temporary point of view, if you will? The poet takes us into a day in which the essential vulnerability of our position is a visceral reality. She invites us to feel and hear and taste the aliveness of right now.

How do we live with impermanence? By adding another layer to the window? By praying for sunnier days? We cannot stop the hail, Rengetsu seems to whisper, but we can be awake. Awake and at peace.

How do you find that peace?

Be yourself. Be yourself, and live that boundless reality intimately, generously, freely. Usually, if you ask someone who they are, you're likely to get the list: "I went to this college, I'm married to this person, I know how to make soup, I'm good at this, I'm bad at that, I can do this, I can do that." We list all the aggregates, all the things that change, all the makeshift identities. But what is the real nature of the self? Noticing the thinness of the seeming barrier between inside and out, just experience that permeability. What are we protecting?

A monk asked Master Tozan, "When heat and cold come, how can we avoid them?" How do we live in this world of trouble, of suffering, of horror, of change, where we can't hold onto what's pleasant or completely get away from what's unpleasant? How can we avoid the heat and cold? Tozan replied, "Go to where there is no heat or cold."

The monk then implored, "But how do I get to that place where there is no heat or cold?" Tozan said, "When it's cold, the cold kills you. When it's hot, the heat kills you." In other words, kill the separation. Quit living in fear of what might be, and dwell in this.

But what about the assault of the hailstones? When what hits is not just weather but something that arrives with intent to harm, what then? I find it inspiring that Rengetsu spends none of the precious moments in her poem cursing the sky, or dissecting the cause of precipitation.

Why are so many people trying to kill so many people? Why is there such enormous greed? Why is there evil? Why did this happen to me? We should consider how a day of hail might be simply, utterly that: a day of hail. Not to be denied, not feared, not hidden from.

There's a story told about an old fisherman out on a very foggy day. Suddenly, this other boat comes and crashes into him. He spends the next couple of hours battening down his boat where it's leaking and cursing this sailor who shouldn't even be on the water, who ruined his day, his catch, his family's meal, and his livelihood. Enraged, he works through the morning, cussing and cursing as, gradually, the fog begins to lift.

Suddenly he sees that what hit him wasn't another boat—it was a rock. All at once, he regrets the hours wasted in such anger, the birds he didn't hear, the enjoyment he didn't feel.

Mountain Retreat in Winter

The little persimmons drying outside
Under the eaves
Of my hermitage
Are they freezing tonight
In the winter storm?

This last of our three poems brings us into the hermitage again, with a feeling of the life under its eaves. Entering the hermitage, in a sense we enter the heart of Buddhism. We stop waiting for company. We stop needing others to show us what's normal, to know what we should do. We sit alone. That's the first teaching gesture of the Buddha: he stopped deferring and referring and looking for an authority. He just sat down—in his own life, in his own mind, in his own condition, with his own karma—and aloneness was transformed. The whole world wasn't excluded; when he sat, the dividing wall between his life, mind, condition, and karma and that of the world was dropped. This is the hermitage heart that beats in each of us. We just need to stop being too afraid to trust it.

Practice is the journey to that trust. It begins when we stop waiting for someone to say: here's the plan, here's the right thing to do, here's the act of courage, of attention, of kindness, of wisdom that you can make. Each of us has that wisdom. Each of us, in fact, is that wisdom. Each of us can leap thoroughly into that hermitage heart and get on with it. We don't need another life, a different condition, a greater wisdom, a better personality. We just need to take care of the life under the eaves of this measureless hermitage.

How? In asking, we begin the journey home.

Sitting in the Dark

From Loren Eiseley's *The Night Country:*

If you cannot bear the silence and the darkness, do not go there; if you dislike black night and yawning chasms, never make them your profession. If you fear the sound of water hurrying through crevices toward unknown and mysterious destinations, do not consider it. Seek out the sunshine. It is a simple prescription. Avoid the darkness.

It is a simple prescription, but you will not follow it. You will turn immediately to the darkness. You will be drawn to it by cords of fear and of longing. You will imagine that you are tired of sunlight; the waters that unnerve you will tug in the ancient recesses of your mind; the midnight will seem restful—you will end by going down.

December 8 is officially recognized as the Buddha's enlightenment day. Zen Buddhists honor it by extending their sitting further and further into the night—for twelve, fourteen, eighteen hours.

How do we understand what all this darkness is about? In one sense, everything we do in Zen Buddhist practice is just what it is—lighting a stick of incense, or bowing, or sitting down and crossing our legs as the evening's shadows deepen around us. It's just that. I'm reminded of the words Minor White used to describe one of his nakedly vibrant photographs: "Not standing for, not metaphor, not thing."

But in another sense, we cannot avoid the discernment process of "Why this, not that?" A mature intelligence will naturally ask that question. So let's consider for a moment what this sitting in the dark—this going off the clock—might be expressing. When we honor the Buddha's enlightenment, what is it that we're honoring? It's easy to have the phrase roll off the tongue, the date roll by on the calendar, and appreciate it as we might, for instance, Halloween. Of course, Halloween doesn't have its core sensibility in non-duality; the tradition of Buddha's enlightenment day does. It may also be tempting to analyze the long hours of sitting as nothing more than spiritual athleticism. I hear variations of this bandied about among Zen students all the time, as if zazen were liver and the harder it is to swallow, the better it must be for you. The more hours on the pillow, the stronger the practitioner. But we can do better than mimicking the Buddha, or trying to prove ourselves by grim willfulness and a racking up of endurance points.

In mystical traditions, real discernment begins by entering a kind of darkness and traveling, figuratively, on a path leading into the night, where things lose their visible distinction, their superficial meaning. Unknowable by definition, this is a path that is not particularly easy, nor strictly sensible. This may be why the weeklong silent meditation retreat known as sesshin is hard to explain to others. If you're talking with somebody who is not in touch with that inner push to sit down with themselves and face the matter of their life and death, you don't want to tell them that you're going to go and stare at the floor for twenty hours a day. They're apt to think perhaps you just need better drugs!

There's an old koan—as there always is—that I call, "The Hot Coal Hidden in the Hearth Ash." It involves Guishan, the

co-founder of the Guiyang School (a school of Zen estab-
lished in the eighth century). Guishan became a monastic at
the age of fifteen, and began study with Baizhang when he
was twenty-four. Early in Guishan's training, according to the
koan, he was sitting in the zendo late into the night—there's
the segue—when his teacher Baizhang saw him and demanded,
"Who is sitting here in the dark?"

Guishan said, 'It's me, master. It's Guishan.'

Baizhang said, 'Rake up the hearth. Stir up the coals.'

Guishan rose, stepped to the hearth, and searched for live
coals but found none. 'The fire is gone out,' he said.

Baizhang then took up the tongs and, deep in the ashes,
found a small, live ember. Holding it up, he said, 'What's this?'

With that, Guishan could acknowledge the live coal of his
own nature, and was deeply enlightened.

Look at the set-up for the interchange in the koan; often
the key to unlocking its heart is implied there. The first thing
we may notice is that Guishan sat alone. He sat unaccompa-
nied. There was no one making it brighter, warmer, friend-
lier—affirming what he was doing.

In the history of Buddhism, we're shown frequent examples of this stalwart aloneness. I think of how Prajapati, the
Buddha's aunt—who had raised him from birth, seen his
transformation, and knew she had to follow suit—left the
comforts and distractions of her royal life and gave herself
utterly to awakening. How she walked 150 miles, barefoot and
bleeding, unstoppable, to pledge herself to the Buddha Way,
only to be told she could not enter. How she persisted. How
solidly she stood in her own calling, unwelcomed into sangha,
yet knowing she was not apart from it. How she made a path
for all who will ever experience the wound of being rejected,
by accepting herself so profoundly. She was followed by hun-
dreds of other women, who undoubtedly were not celebrated
in their families and communities for taking such bold steps.
Each of them had to walk alone, even though their footsteps

combined to raise quite a lot of dust. Sometimes, I think we can sniff the air even now and get a little whiff of it.

Aloneness—getting to that Prajapati kind of walking, that Guishan style of sitting—is by no means easy. I still remember the sensation in my body when I heard, at the ripe old age of thirteen, of Paul's instructions in the Bible that women should not speak in church. I could not articulate the pain, and would not know the magnitude of the silencing for years, but I sat there and slowly crumpled and twisted in my fingers a small booklet as the minister spoke. It's striking to me how palpable the feeling of that twisted paper booklet in my hand remains when I return in memory to that morning. Not that I had a great aspiration to speak in a church (or a zendo!). In fact, I was so shy I could barely speak at the dinner table. But I knew I was somehow unwelcome in what I had presumed was the place of unconditional welcome. It can take years to recover the natural, steady confidence that is our birthright. Prajapati makes a call for women, particularly, that we can, and need to, welcome ourselves into the journey. As does Guishan.

He is in the dark. He can't see. He doesn't know. What kind of darkness is Guishan in? This is the next key to the koan, to seeing how it might open what's locked within us. So let's look into the matter of darkness itself.

Probably the easiest appropriation of darkness, one that we're familiar with by habit, is the darkness of simple dimwittedness. We just don't get it. We just don't notice that there's a great matter at hand: that we were mysteriously born, that we're dying. And in the effort to spare us from wasting our time (or perhaps just to give us the pleasure of good company), there are Buddhist teachings that show how common basic spiritual dimwittedness has always been.

One of my favorites likens Zen students to different kinds of horses. There's a horse that only gallops when the whip touches bone. These kinds of students are the ones who wait until the moment of their death to realize that they're dying, and that there's an implicit question or imperative in their being. It takes that long. It has to come that close.

Then there's the kind of horse that only moves, only runs, only begins to awaken, when the whip breaks the flesh. And this is likened to the students who begin to move in practice, begin to come to awakening, when there is a death in their family. It's getting near. It's come into the house. It can't quite be ignored.

The metaphor keeps going. There's the horse that only moves, only runs, only begins to love and awaken, when the whip touches the skin. This is like those students who begin their spiritual life when there is death in their neighborhood, when epidemics break out, when the buildings fall, when the threat is implicit in culture.

And then there's the horse that moves at the shadow of the whip—the most highly regarded Zen student, for whom the smallest indication gives the fullest implication. The most infinitesimal movement of consciousness, of being, implies all movement, all coming and going, all life and death: the basic issue at hand. Those students are ripe, so primed for whatever's required, whatever's calling, that they're completely available, completely present.

And then—as my teacher, Daido Roshi, always used to add when he'd talk of the horses—there is the dead horse. Nothing, nothing moves them. Roshi would laugh, but there wasn't anyone who didn't feel the jab. It's not hard to spend a sitting period complaining aimlessly to yourself about the weather and the trivial, inviting that dead-horse stench to fill the nostrils.

Dimwittedness, spiritual or otherwise, is always much easier to point out in others than it is to see in oneself. It's so widespread, the tendency to check out of our responsibilities, our world, our possibilities. A recent study revealed that only thirteen percent of high school students can find Iraq on a world map. Very few of us, even in this age of information, really understand that when the African continent is dying, we are dying. That given the ongoing degradation and commod- ification of water resources, within decades constant thirst will be the norm for most of the earth's population. The whip has already penetrated the skin. We should not wait for bone.

Many who are committed to the Buddhist tradition sim- ply don't allow to register in their hearts, for instance, the reality of how Asian women's lives are impacted by religious discrimination. Sandy Boucher outlines the situation in *Open- ing the Lotus: A Woman's Guide to Buddhism*: "There are about sixty thousand women in the Buddhist tradition, mostly Asian women, who call themselves nuns, wear robes, and live a renunciant's life, but most have not received the full authoriz- ation of their tradition. Thus many of the women who have dedicated their entire lives to the Dharma are denied the material support of the sangha, kept from the teachings and instruction they need, and treated like servants and religious nonentities." What is our responsibility, our imperative, once we know?

Besides dimwittedness, darkness can also indicate depres- sion, a lack of hope, perhaps even despair. We go dark when we've concluded in our heart-mind-body that it's a lose-lose game, being alive. You try hard, you love hard, you give fully— and you lose. People die, your best efforts fail, you put yourself into the work and the work doesn't produce results. And so you despair. You decide, "This is reality. And I don't want to play." Of course, not playing is also losing, because you're still alive. And every moment you're not living your life, you're losing it.

Sitting in the dark of depression and despair is sitting with conclusions—or the emotional residue of those conclusions. Many Zen students who are usually resilient dabble with this quality of darkness. They're exhausted from the effort to improve the state of things, only to see injustice and greed seemingly trammel all hope. So they come to quiet conclusions, and light dims in the eyes. There's a kind of seeping fog through which many are viewing the future.

Once such a depression really gets hold, we often don't even know it has any underpinnings in thought; the thoughts have created a body of despair. Energy seems unavailable to even investigate the reality we've created; it seems like the way things really are. And so part of what we need to see as we work with this is: what is it to sit in that darkness? What is it to practice spiritual life in such a way that we see those quiet, unspoken assumptions about reality? That we see if they're true, see if they hold—and if not, get clear.

In John Hull's poignant and powerful book, *Touching the Rock: An Experience of Blindness*, he expresses many acute observations about what it is like to go blind. At one point he asks, "Was there a meaning in it? Was I meant to go blind? People often ask me questions like these. My blindness was the result of thousands of tiny accidental happenings. These were not a 'path' and I was not being led along it towards blindness. Looking back, I can see the chain of events, and it looks a bit like a path, but any trackless waste is laid out with paths once it has been crossed. When you look ahead, there is no path but only an almost infinite number of possibilities."

His is not a sentimental resolve; he never ignores the fact that many of the steps ahead might be difficult. What I take great strength from is his unwavering sense of the hugeness of what is ahead, and how the attraction of its mystery isn't stained with what seems to be any sense of dread.

Back to Guishan. He was not considered a bright light. This was not someone about whom everyone at the monastery buzzed, "Hey, this kid. He's got great, great promise. Gonna do big things in the Dharma, this one is." He was kind of a fuddy-duddy himself. How did it happen that he became one of the greatest hearts on the planet? Someone whose words, whose actions, whose gestures in a small building on a mountaintop in China would come to shake the world? To penetrate through time, to here and now, to this moment when things seem so dark?

Perhaps Guishan was sitting where there is no distinction. Perhaps his sitting was the intimate expression of enlightenment, so close to the heart of things that no observation was possible, no distance was necessary. That darkness, which is the absolute nature of reality, the nature of each one of us, may be where this monastic was sitting.

His teacher had to challenge it, to check it out: Are you just punked out, depressed? Avoiding the other monastics? Can't sleep because you face your despair if you close your eyes? Or are you sitting in the darkness of profound intimacy, in which sleeping and waking, self and other, doing and not doing, are not apart from one another? What about this? So Baizhang calls out to him, "Who is sitting here? Who *are* you?"

Of course, this is what every element of Zen training is always asking. If it's not asking that of you, then you're not engaging Zen training. If you're learning a gig—how to sit and not be yelled at, how to do a liturgy and get it right, how to fit in—you've turned it all into some seventh-grade test. That's not why you came to the threshold of the zendo and entered.

To create an environment of Zen training is to let it hold you dynamically in the question of your self nature. The environment itself encourages you not to fall into despair or prolonged depression. Nor to fall into answer, truth, knowing. What is it to really live? Who is sitting here in the dark?

Guishan says, "It's Guishan, master. It's me."

And so, to meet Baizhang and Guishan intimately— to see what they're teaching, why their story is repeated, recorded, presented as a way to wake up—we need to see what this reply is.

If this is your student, and you say to him, "Who are you, sitting here in the dark?" and the student answers, "It's me, Guishan," is that student clear and free and at home in reality?

He might be saying, "There's only Guishan. I can't find anything but Guishan here. Wherever I look, wherever I breathe, whatever I think, wherever I go, it's nothing but Guishan." That would be one thing.

But he could also just be caught up in his name. And most of us are caught up in names for ourselves and for things and for one another. Whether that name is "teacher" or "student" or "hero" or "idiot," we believe it. We identify ourselves with it. With these names, we make the world according to our ideas. We may even make God with a name, and while we're at it, we make him male. There are consequences to the names we give, gaps created into which suffering rises like storm water. Real people drown in that water. Life is absolutely at stake. Your life, mine, the life of this entire planet, now that we're a global community.

So, what is Guishan saying? The teacher presses him: make it clear to me if it's clear to you. He says, "Rake up the hearth." Show me the light in the darkness. Show me the fact that if this darkness actually contains all things, it doesn't negate light. Show me.

He's raking up the hearth just by asking, but Guishan doesn't see that. Instead, he gets up, steps to the hearth, and searches for live coals—but finds none. "The fire's gone out," Guishan says. And again, we face a question: what is finding no coals? It's still not completely evident. Has the fire of self-centered desire been put out? Perhaps this is the same realization that Patacara, the female elder from the Buddha's time, the most cited teacher of the Therigatha, pointed to in her enlightenment poem translated by Susan Murcott:

Then I took a lamp,
and went into my cell,
checked the bed,
and sat down on it.
I took a needle

and pushed the wick down.

When the lamp went out,
My mind was freed.

But Guishan still can't make it clear; he can't remove all doubt. He's stuck on one side: form is emptiness. Baizhang suddenly gets up, digs into the ash himself, reaches into the place where there is nothing, and picks up something. He holds up the glowing coal—emptiness is form—and asks, "What about this?"

A superficial grasping of the koan turns it into simply a call to "dig deeper." But if that were its whole import, it would be nothing more than a slogan. What is it to reach into that darkness with your sitting, with your practice, without knowing, without needing it to be done and over? "I found the fire. Now I'm awake. Now my thirst is sated. Now I'm warmed by reality. Time is over."

We need to see both sides: the fire is dead, and the coal is alive. Without desire, I vow to put an end to desires. Without light, I vow to bring light wherever it is needed. It seems to be a contradiction. But contradictions take place in language, not in reality.

What is the reality? How will you rake the hearth? What ember will you offer, from deep within the ash, to all those who are sitting alone in the night?

Small Matters

Seventy-two labors brought us this food; we should know how it comes to us. Zen Buddhists say a version of the gatha (or chant) before every meal. How does it come to us? By *seventy-two labors:* the effort of server, cook, farmer. The community working together brings it to this bowl: the teacher training students, the administrator managing the office, the one cleaning the floor, making the bed, painting the sign. Seventy-two, I was told, was the number of work positions in a traditional monastery. It must have been a large place, a place where you didn't notice the twenty-seventh monk, or the fifty-third. Each meal is an occasion to remember even those we don't see bring us this food. Every effort contributes.

Today, it's easy not to notice—not to notice the lives of cattle, the chickens' crowded cages, the small farmer's struggle. It can seem so complicated and sad, knowing how the meal comes to us. Still, there are the sheer places. Years ago, paddling a canoe down Long Pond in the Catskills, I came to where an old apple tree held its fruit out over the water. I plucked an apple seemingly offered—from a tree planted who knows how long ago—by someone long gone. *We should know how it comes to us.* As one of my teachers, Maezumi Roshi, used to put it, "Let us appreciate."

35

When I was sixteen and dating for the first time, my mother counseled me: "Watch how a man treats a waitress and you'll see who he really is." It took me a long time to understand what was important in her words. The way we receive the gifts of this life reveals who we are. Some won't even notice they are being served. Some will think it their due. And some will know gratitude as a generally apt response to the matter at hand.

The container corresponds to the amount put in. That's the definition we usually hear of *oryoki*, the ritual meal we eat in Zen training. The emphasis here is on what we put in—and the size of our life will correspond to that effort. So often, the training imperative is: "Really put yourself into it!" When you do that in liturgy, reality becomes immeasurable. When you do that in zazen, it becomes limitless.

But if the amount put in creates the size of our life, then the size of our life also creates the amount put in. It's an equation you can approach from either side. The larger the container, the larger the offering. As Charlotte Joko Beck put it in her wonderful "ABC" teaching, if we are "A Bigger Container," we receive more of the meal. If we are the great Earth itself, every kindness shown is shown to us. We become lucky.

As we receive this offering, we should consider whether our virtue and practice deserve it. A hard point, a chewy chant. How do you deserve an offering, earn the gift of life? The wave of self-esteem rises and falls—of course we deserve to be nourished, and of course our virtue is lacking. How many are hungry in the world right now? Are they less deserving than the well fed? The flavor here is subtle. The teaching in this part of the meal gatha is simply, "we should consider." Just that. Get present. This moment now is where virtue and practice are realized. Don't get lost in the past. Just consider. Don't get lost in promises about the future. (I'll do better, really I will!)

Just consider.

There's a haunting image in a short story in a collection by Thomas Vasseur. A grieving father of a lost baby finds, in a garbage bag, "the yellow crib blanket his aunt had crocheted, tumbled in with cantaloupe peels, paper towels soaked with bacon grease, coffee grounds and the empty Raisin Bran box he'd left on the kitchen table the night before." And in another story, a divorced man's young son rests his head on his father's shoulder during a long flight to take the boy back to his mother. Vasseur writes, "Drops of sweet-pungent baby sweat formed on his temples. How his father would miss that smell! Only a few days from now, Mark would find one of Sam's T-shirts in the laundry, bury his nose in it, then place it in the chest of drawers unwashed." No one in these stories can hold onto what they love. None of us can. Call it vulnerability, or simply the nature of being. Still, loss arrives at the breakfast table. It's in the laundry basket. It's in the heart-mind of being alive. We don't get to skip this. How we live it is, in a sense, everything.

What is deserved? Verdant, composting—what is this strange mulch of loving and leaving, with always a scent in the air of an unnameable longing? We all know there's more to this meal than apples in the sun.

Being the world, we also receive every cruelty. The great first-cenury lay practitioner Vimalakirti said of his sickness, "If any sentient being is sick, I am sick." Buddha said of his awakening, "I and all sentient beings are simultaneously enlightened." Both instruct us not to set ourselves apart. Even as we are inexplicably fortunate, we find the yellow blankets of our missing loved ones stained and abandoned with the remnants of yesterday's meal. The meal chant implores us: don't skim over it or slide away from it. Consider. We are capable of this immense and poignant consideration. And that consideration is practice itself.

In *For the Time Being*, Annie Dillard wondered about what matters. She wrote, "One small town's soup kitchen, St. Mary's, serves about 115 men a night. Why feed 115 individuals? Surely so few people elude most demographics and achieve statistical insignificance. After all, there are 270 million Americans, 19 million people who live in greater New York, 26 million in greater Tokyo. Every day, 1.5 million people walk through Times Square in New York; every day, almost as many people—1.5 million—board U.S. passenger planes. And so forth. We who breathe air now will join the already dead layers of us who breathed air once. We arise from dirt, and dwindle to dirt, and the might of the universe is arrayed against us." She also reflected, "The early Amish in this country used to roll their community's dead bodies in wraps of sod before they buried them. We are food, like rolled sandwiches, for the Greek god Chronos, time, who eats his children." Her food image goes right to the belly. What is the practice of being food for time, and deserving the food of this moment? To genuinely consider this, without lapsing into anxiety or apology, may be virtue enough.

As we desire the natural order of mind, to be free from clinging we must be free from greed. Since clinging and greed are only a shade or two awayt from being the same thing, the prescription in this part of the chant calls for us to swallow what may be the most difficult pill of all: to be free, what we have to do is be free. The natural mind is free; freedom is the natural mind. But being free in our mind means we can't be victims any more. We no longer have the excuse of being restricted, controlled, or dominated.

But we are locked up—in jails, in bodies that age and break down. How do we realize freedom in prison?

In order to work on our greed and clinging, we have to realize that it comes from our fear. We live afraid we'll be struck down again, or afraid we'll lose whatever it is that allows us relative privilege or safety. Afraid the pain will be larger than

bearable, or afraid death will be more a mean thing than a
mystery. And so we cling.

A friend whose son designs handbags said he told her that
ninety-three percent of Japanese women between age twenty
and forty own Louis Vuitton handbags. "Can you believe it?"
she asked. "It makes me sad." I don't know what these handbags are, what they mean. Do the seven percent without them
know a taste of freedom the ninety-three percent have only
the most vague dreams of? What we carry is so often the ico-
nography of who we want to be: loved by the children whose
pictures are in the wallet, ready with pens for a poem to arrive
and make us poets, or a cell phone to ring with the critical
business to which only we can attend—and only now.

Tim O'Brien's *The Things They Carried* is widely considered to be the definitive fictional account of the American
soldiers' experience in Vietnam and a landmark in American
literary form. Years ago I jotted down a passage from an inter-
view in which he said, "When I wrote *The Things They Carried*
about going to war for fear of embarrassment, I wanted people
to love me, like me—my country, people in my home town,
my mom and my dad. Really central to me, more than war, are
the things human beings will do for love." To want love is the
natural order of mind—notice that this morsel of the chant
begins, "as we desire." But to need love at all expense, to con-
tort, control, and cling—that is the mind of fear, the illness
we're here to heal.

To support our life we take this food. How large is our life? Here's
a story told to me by a cab driver while we were talking about
how you never know: "I was all dressed up, heading out for a
nice dinner. It was last December; real snowy like it was all
month. I see this lady with a flat tire out there trying to change
it in the middle of the road, and she was pregnant, all alone. So
I change the tire for her. She offers me money and I say, 'Now,

don't go insulting me, lady.' Someone in her condition, you know, she shouldn't be changing a tire out there in the snow. Well, about four months later, I'm in this store downtown to get some clothes, and I've got a pile of shirts and socks I take up to the cash register. The guy behind the register says, 'Sir, I can't let you buy these.' I ask him, kind of in a huff, just exactly why not, and he points to this lady across the room and says, 'Do you recognize that lady?' I don't, and then he says, 'Well, that's my wife, and you changed her tire in a snowstorm a couple months back. This is my store, and these clothes are on the house, sir. I can't thank you enough.' Now, wasn't that something?"

The often-overlooked twenty-seventh monk, I think, laboring away in the side streets of this boundless monastery.

Tang Dynasty Master Xuefeng, teaching his community, said, "Pick up the whole great earth in your fingers, and it's as big as a grain of rice. Throw it down before you. If, like a lacquer bucket, you don't understand, I'll beat the drum to call everyone to look." This is spiritual obesity: consuming the whole earth in each meager grain, manifesting a body so vast there is no place to put it because there is no place it does not reach. Instead of beating ourselves up for our overconsumption, indulging ourselves with perpetual guilt, here's the alternative: receive the offering and support life with it. If we don't get it, Xuefeng will be beating that drum, and before we get over being humiliated, the last fruit may fall from the last tree.

Supporting life is also just practical, and good for everybody. A recent report in the *American Journal of Public Health* found, for instance, that higher income inequality is associated with increased mortality at all per capita income levels. In other words, the less we share the meal, the more folks die, regardless of their place at the table. From this dry report so full of juice: "Given the mortality burden associated with income inequality, business, private, and public sector initiatives to reduce economic inequalities should be a high prior-

ity." Ultimately, there's no advantage to starving the left side of
the body while feeding the right: the whole body tumbles
together into the heap. We might as well feed one another.
That's news to pass around.

To attain our way we take this food. What is "our way"? Let's
appreciate the question for a moment. The body hasn't tumbled yet. There is still the occasional apple, and maybe—just
maybe—you or I have an undeniably important role in
whether a child born a hundred years from now will know its
sweet taste, and how the clean, cool air opens the senses. What
is it to sit, an apple on an outstretched branch, perfect in its
imperfect roundness, offering this? "Zazen," Zen Master
Dogen said, "isn't step-by-step meditation; it is simply the
dharma gate to peace and joy. It is both the practice and the
realization of totally culminated enlightenment." Perhaps all
religious life will keep coming back to the issue of an apple.
Wouldn't that be something?

Threshold

What is the gate of Zen? Is there a way to live in the threshold of every moment? Pablo Neruda wrote in the opening stanzas of his verse, "Poetry" in this version translated by Alastair Reid:

> *And it was at that age...Poetry arrived*
> *in search of me. I don't know, I don't know where*
> *it came from, from winter or a river.*
> *I don't know how or when,*
> *no they were not voices, they were not*
> *words, nor silence,*
> *but from a street I was summoned,*
> *from the branches of night,*
> *abruptly from the others,*
> *among violent fires*
> *or returning alone,*
> *there I was without a face*
> *and it touched me.*

In meditation practice, we explore this threshold, this place where old and new meet in a body. Tonight as we sit until midnight on this cusp of the New Year, the natural question of this meeting place becomes our focus. We explore the "liminal"—the realm in which we're touched beyond personality, beyond the limits of what we understand or have assigned ourselves as our life. A practitioner of Zen is most basically one whose life is awakening each moment to that threshold, the still point where all the possibilities exist. To practice is to release oneself from the momentum of the past, the karma of what seems to be indicated as the only next step. It is to turn one's face toward the unknown as a way of life.

I recall Maezumi Roshi once saying, "Once through the gate, the discovery is made that the gate is not actually a barrier or an opening through which to pass. It's simply reality presenting itself." Usually we either regard that barrier gate, that threshold, as a place of stopping or as a place of incipient going. Maezumi Roshi pointed to the place where there is neither coming nor going, neither speech nor silence—no momentum, and yet utter obligation to all things. This is what touched Neruda. But what is it?

The anthropologist Victor Turner also took up that moment at the threshold in his book *Ritual Process: Structure and Anti-Structure*. He described it as "the liminal—the time and space of transition integral to all rites of passage. Entering this condition, a person leaves behind his or her old identity and dwells in a threshold state of ambiguity, openness and indeterminacy." It's easy to see that every Zen koan, in a sense, is simply that: "Entering... a threshold state of ambiguity, openness and indeterminacy...." In other words, not knowing. Every liturgy is that liminal realm. Everything, every breath, is the threshold.

What tends to happen as we become used to—or familiar with—the language and devices of Zen, its rhetoric of gates and barriers, is that we cease to recognize what its real demand is, what its real offering is. What happened when Neruda entered this state in which he surrendered his path, his direction? When he was summoned from the street, from where he thought he was heading, from what he thought he was doing? Suddenly, his life was up for grabs—his face was missing, his identity couldn't be found, and that allowed a life larger than his own to touch him. A life beyond his agenda, his ideas, began at that moment. But at the root of all the gate-barrier-threshold teachings is the essential question, "What is it that touches the mind at such a moment?"

Surrendering path and face, letting go of our self-ideas about direction: how is that accomplished? Ambiguity may not seem so attractive when we're craving certainty as if it were water. Allowing reality to arrive, or as Maezumi Roshi said, "to present itself," isn't easy. The fact that we can't grasp or guarantee it is reality's challenge. To live in that threshold, to let one's life be that threshold itself, is to not be dependent on the temporary comforts of knowing something, of being someone, of going somewhere. This is why practice can be so fundamentally uncomfortable: until we let go, we are holding on, and that hurts.

We can see the challenge of the threshold in the life of Patacara, who lived in India at the time of the Buddha. Patacara was a very strong young woman. When her parents picked out a prospective husband for her, she secretly married a servant who had long been her lover. In this detail, we get an indication that she was, from the beginning, not much of a rule-follower. The consequence of that allegiance to her own heart was rejection by her family. She and her husband had to leave and make their home in a distant part of India.

It was the custom in that culture for a woman to return to her mother's house when it was time to give birth. When her first child was due, Patacara was delayed by her husband in starting her journey, and gave birth in the woods. When she was pregnant the second time, her husband was again resistant, so she began the trek without him. He soon followed, and found his family deep in the forest as a fierce storm began kicking up. As he gathered timber to build a shelter for his child and pregnant wife, he was bitten by a snake and died. Patacara gave birth alone. She sheltered her newborn and her other child with her body as the storm raged on.

In grief over her husband's unexpected death, Patacara realized that she and her children would no longer be welcome in his village. Her only option was to proceed to her parents' home and beg to be welcomed. To get there, she had to cross a large river, now a torrent because of the storm.

Unable to make the crossing with both children, she told the toddler to stay put and entered the water carrying the newborn. She crossed the river, settled the newborn into a nest of leaves, and began to make her way back for her other child. But when she reached mid-river, to her horror, she saw a hawk swoop down, pick up the infant, and begin carrying it away. She cried out, trying to get the hawk to release her baby, but it ignored her. Her older child, hearing her shriek, thought his mother was calling him to come to her. He ran into the water toward her, and she watched as he was swept up in the current and drowned.

Like Job, Patacara is brought to a level of sadness so low it is hard to imagine. Somehow, she made her way out of the river and continued walking toward her old home. Along the road, she met someone from the town, and asked them about her family. This person told her that during the storm, her family's house collapsed and they were killed. Patacara went mad with grief, and no longer tried to protect herself. She wandered—naked, disheveled, disoriented.

So far, the story is largely about what happened to Patacara, but let's look at what she did, instead. She had lived according to her heart, and persevered against all odds. And now she had exhausted all reference systems, if you will. Nothing protected her from suffering, and she knew it. She now saw through all the things that had been of value to her. No one could get near her. She saw every offer of false hope for what it was. "I'll take care of you" was no longer a promise she could believe. "I'll be there for you"—she knew that no one could guarantee that. All the games were over. In the most profound sense, she was naked.

Unwilling, or perhaps no longer able, to submit to the conventions that enabled fitting into her culture, she kept wandering. When she came upon Jeta Grove, where the Buddha was teaching, his disciples found her appearance to be frightening and appalling. But when the Buddha saw her, he rose and followed her. He placed himself in her path and when they met, said, "Sister, it is time to recover your presence of mind." Patacara came to her senses, realized she was naked, and gratefully covered herself with a cloak. Then she asked the Buddha for help.

It's important to recognize what's happening in this story. It's easy to say that the Buddha did something, gave Patacara something. But realize that she heard not simply the words of Shakyamuni Buddha, but the timeless Buddha voice that calls us to wake up, to recover our presence of mind. She heard her first Dharma talk, if you will. And she had emptied herself so completely of games and illusions that she could hear it.

After listening to Patacara's tragic story, the Buddha told her that throughout her many lives, she "had shed more tears for the loss of loved ones than there was water in the oceans." This, too, is critical. In her hearing of the Buddha voice, we can see what happens when our life is recognized. The Buddha mind meets us in our suffering, when we drop all the devices we use to buffer ourselves against it.

Then the Buddha reminded her, "At your death, even had they all been living, your family could only look on in helpless despair. Only the dharma can help you." Hearing this, Patacara decided to ordain and was taken into the nun's community, which welcomed her.

What did she realize? The Buddha told Patacara, "Recover your presence of mind." What happens when we ordain into the truth of this boundless mind itself? When we recognize that no one can help us come home because we've never left? Patacara was freed.

She went on to become a great teacher. She had thirty disciples, which for a woman of her time was pretty odd. She is, in a sense, the star of the Therigatha, the enlightenment poems of the Buddhist nuns and laywomen. Her voice appears in the collection more often than any other. In her poem, translated by Susan Murcott, which gives us an indication of what she realized, she says:

> *I took a needle*
> *and pushed the wick down.*
> *When the lamp went out,*
> *My mind was freed.*

It's akin to what we encounter in Neruda's absent face, that sheerness and daily-ness, that everything-ness of awakening. "Show me your face before your parents were born," the famous koan asks. "For Neruda," the poet and essayist Jane Hirshfield wrote in *Nine Gates: Entering the Mind of Poetry*, "that face becomes a poetry of all things: a long praise-song to salt in the mines and in the ocean, to a wristwatch ticking in the night's darkness like a tiny saw cutting time, to the dead body of a fish in the market. In the light of the poet's abundance of heart and imagination, we remember the threshold is a place at once empty and full. It is on the margins, where one thing meets another, and in the times of transition, that ecosystems are most rich and diverse—birds sing, and deer, fish, and mosquitoes emerge to feed at dawn and at dusk."

But at such a threshold, we're not sure of that richness. We're not sure of mosquitoes. We're not sure of deer or stars.

We're not sure of anything. We're just, as the anthropologist Turner said, "in a state of ambiguity, openness and indeterminacy." We're in a state of beginner's mind. We're in a state of self-forgetting, that state which the Buddha called "presence of mind." It's almost redundant: recover your presence, and recover your mind. Don't "know" about your situation. Be profoundly present.

"Only afterward," Turner wrote, "may the initiate enter into new forms of identity and relationship, rejoining the everyday life of the culture—but now as an adult or married person, as healer or holder of clan secrets." This is the ritual process of the threshold, celebrated in a marriage ceremony, in taking the Buddhist vows, in committing to being a student. When may we initiate the new forms of relationship? When we've forgotten the self, when we've dropped the face, when all relationships are transformed, all things are radiant.

But our transitions trigger a great deal of initial fear; we feel like we're going to somehow fall apart if we go forward. That's why steps seem so hard to take before we take them. A wonderful martial arts teacher of mine once counseled several of us who were pulling back, saying that we had to practice in class just as we'd practiced learning how to walk. In order to walk, a child needs to first develop a willingness to fall, because walking is nothing but falling and recovering. If willingness to fall isn't there, you just never give walking a shot. Life crawls on, but you never really become an upright human being.

The willingness to step into the unknown and possibly take a fall is to surrender to the threshold. When what's falling is everyone you love, or your sense of your self, or your direction—life in the liminal calls us from the street. To let it touch us, we have to practice our fears.

In the Buddhist scripture collection known as the Abhidharma, five great fears are listed. Since I first read that list, I've often reflected on how whatever fear I had coming up might fit into this ancient system.

1 – fear of death
2 – fear of the loss of livelihood
3 – fear of unusual states of consciousness
4 – fear of loss of reputation
5 – fear of speaking before a public assembly

What are we afraid of? The uncountable millions of things—from the mystery of mortality, to the intractable sense of loss when there is no one to love or no one to love us, to the abuses of cruel people, or an indifferent, chaotic world. But right in that moment of fear is the place where either life becomes a threshold, or a curse. Daido Roshi often said, "If you miss the moment, you miss your life." We don't need a grand plan: "I'll live my life as a threshold." It's enough to practice now. It's enough to practice this. "You have cried more tears than there is water in the ocean," the Buddha said. He began his teaching there, with the recognition that life is suffering, fearful, plagued by insatiable thirsts. "It is time to recover your presence of mind," the Buddha continued. It is time. Not Patacara's time; your time; my time. Not later, not when we feel differently.

A few years ago I was visiting with my mom, who lived in an apartment complex that increasingly housed solitary elderly women. They blew my heart open, because in one sense you could look at them and just see a fabric of misery. Here were the broken hip and the arthritis, the diabetes and the widowhood and the uncaring children... It was almost overwhelming. But then it dawned on me how every day, every moment, they had not opted for any of the not-so-difficult-to-figure-out exits. You know: leap off the tenth floor, and stop this story. And they stayed in a kind of attention to, "What about today? What's at this threshold?" They didn't say it like that. They'd think that was the corniest, stupidest thing they'd ever heard.

But they breathed it. They lived it. They showed it.

A number of specific characteristics mark this state of being "betwixt and between" in the liminal world. Again, Turner, the anthropologist, explains that first, the initiate undergoes the removal of identity and status, becoming nameless; conventional clothing is foregone; the usual constraints of gender no longer apply. And this is ritualized in the receiving of the robe in Zen training. It's obvious in the story of Patacara shedding her clothes, her currency of communicating appropriateness or protection.

Ordinarily forbidden behavior is now allowed, or, conversely, the person may enter into an extreme discipline equally foreign to conventional life. Like attending one's mind, not running from every discomfort. Often there is a period of silence, of non-doing, of fasting or going without sleep. Threshold persons are treated as outsiders and exiles, separated from the group, reviled, ignored. The Zen monk leaves home, becoming *unsui*, Japanese for "clouds and water." This was Patacara with no place to land. In a way, it is the gesture of being in intense meditation practice—removing yourself from that street, dwelling in mystery, willing to be misunderstood by those who do not understand why you'd do such a thing.

Possessing nothing, they descend into invisibility and darkness, and—symbolically or literally abandoning both the physical and the ideological structures of society for a wilderness existence. The desert fathers entered the desert; the forest monks and nuns entered the forest. This is the wilderness in which there is no path. There's no guidance in the true wilderness. We create the superstructure of training to hold and encourage that liminal life—come see the teacher, come hear the talk—but in fact there is nothing that a teacher can give you. Why? Because you are already whole. Patacara was already whole. That's why when encouraged—when sparked—by the Buddha's words, "Recover your presence of mind," she could.

It's why when a teacher says, "Trust yourself," you can.

I'd like to end as I began, with a poem. Jane Hirshfield wrote, in a piece called "Late Prayer," of a time of difficulty—when she was struggling to invoke, to invite, to pray for the Bodhi mind of living in the threshold:

> *Tenderness does not choose its own uses.*
> *It goes out to everything equally,*
> *circling rabbit and hawk.*
> *Look: in the iron bucket,*
> *a single nail, a single ruby —*
> *all the heavens and hells.*
> *They rattle in the heart and make one sound.*

We don't get to choose whether it's ruby or nail, whether it's kindness and grace and flow, or abuse and pain and awkwardness. What we can ordain into is that it's one sound in the heart. It's one threshold. It's one moment. May we recover it in presence of mind.

Cold Mountain Home

In honor of the extraordinary weather we've had during recent winters—forecasters noted that for the first times in years we experienced what they call "snow thunder"—I'd like to dedicate this chapter to the great recluse, the Cold Mountain poet Han-shan (Tang Dynasty 618-90).

I like my home being well hidden
a dwelling place cut off from the world's noise and dust
trampling the grass has made three paths
looking up at the clouds makes neighbors in the four directions
there are birds to help with the sound of singing
but there isn't anyone to ask about the words of the Dharma.
today among these withered trees
how many years make one spring

January, the beginning of the new year, shares some features with the beginning month of any *ango*—the ninety-day training intensive at Zen Buddhist monasteries. Both inspire an initial burst of commitment and vision followed by the settling down to the "dire" day-to-day work of actually keeping our vows. And once that first burst of possibly romantic energy wanes, there can be some serious disappointment as our seeming failures mount and our freshness fades. It's easy to create hiding places within ourselves, places that give us some sense of temporary relief, but Han-shan celebrates a wonderfully different kind of sanctuary.

In winter the declining light, the increasing cold, the longer hours of darkness may bring to mind death and the encroaching of the unknowable. Cultures worldwide have recognized this "January quality" in literature, poetry, and religious ritual. Warm is what a living human body is; cold is what a dead human body is. Warm sings of vitality; cold carries an unspeakable sense of vulnerability.

If we are self-conscious, we may become awkward and subtly angry at being so exposed. Or we may become so self-forgetting that we experience awakening with the sudden sound of snow crunching. Because the self-conscious and the self-forgetting dwell together—not infrequently in one body—January is often a time when the psychological and social intensities of Zen training are keenly experienced. Depressed, numb moods arise. Criticisms and judgments of oneself and others come into full flower. Severe doubts dwell together in the mind and on the same mountain with the simple, sheer wonder at all the ways those months are filled with generosity. At the same time a state of exceptional rawness and honesty often enters the community or sangha. We find we need to tread carefully with each other and perhaps bring more tenderness to bear in our interactions.

Han-shan literally means "Cold Mountain." Like many Chinese teachers of his time, he took the name of the place where he lived. This practice harkens to a time when where you were and who you were had a recognized, intrinsic connection. Robert Aiken Roshi once said that Han-shan and another poet, Shi-te, "epitomized the sangha, the coming together of creative, illumined minds. One lived in a cave, the other was a cook's helper in a monastery. Both were considered crazy by people we have long forgotten." Not much more is known about Han-Shan; what we do know is constructed from his poems, which were collected by a late-ninth-century Zen master.

As Han-shan's poem begins:

I like my home being well hidden.
A dwelling place cut off
from the world's noise and dust.

These lines describe the mountain cave where Han-shan lived, and the simple fact that he liked it. But the practice that is revealed in those words also invites us to appreciate the lines as having deeper potential, as pointing to a home harder to recognize, the dwelling place we perhaps call "our own mind." This home is not obvious because it cannot be grasped. Look for it and it cannot be found.

This is the same point made in the interchange between the great sixth-century Chinese Buddhist monk Bodhidharma and his disciple Huike. Arriving at a cave where Bodhidharma sat facing the wall, Huike begged to be relieved of his suffering. Bodhidharma ignored him. As it snowed through the night, Huike was unswerving in his appeal, in his steadfastness. He sat still as the snow deepened all around him. Finally Bodhidharma noticed that in Huike lived the heart of a real student. He said, "What have you come for? Why are you here?" Huike said, "My mind is not at peace. Please, set it at peace for me." Bodhidharma said, "Bring me your mind and I will set it at peace for you." And Huike looked for the mind. The accounts don't tell us for how many hours or minutes or days or months, but simply that Huike looked exhaustively— as exhaustively as it is possible to look. Finally he returned to Bodhidharma, spread his arms wide, and said, "I have looked for the mind and I cannot grasp it." Bodhidharma said, "There, I've set it at peace for you."

This peace of mind that is our true home—the dwelling place that is not constructed out of dust and noise and distraction—is our birthright. Yet we live in an increasingly noisy world. The technologies of information and influence are definitely sophisticated. More and more people have fallen prey to the notion that being "smart consumers" is the same thing as being intelligent, responsible human beings. The forces of greed are so compelling, so well-funded, so articulate in how conditioning works that an ever-greater number of us are actually devoting a large part of our lives not only to consuming, but to *becoming* brands or products, to becoming some advertising executive's idea of strong and sexy, masculine or feminine, youthful, groomed, smart. Having accomplished that, we become desirable commodities. It sneaks up on us, and infects how we live, and how we understand and love one another.

Consider the often-slanted presentation of Zen adepts in modern Buddhist literature. These heroic figures are ever-serene, resourceful, contented, disciplined, and spontaneous. They never fret about the cost or the pain of a weeklong meditation retreat. They never face economic, political, and social barriers to training. Why? If we do not see each other's struggles and victories as inspiration, we may just conclude, "They are good; we are bad." That conclusion separates us from the truth of our lives and invites suffering to pour into our minds.

Enlightenment is not a competition. Suffering is not a competition. Isn't it time to stop measuring whose suffering is worse, whose enlightenment is biggest—to cut the noise? Let's just practice—let's practice not measuring each other or patronizing each other. Let's sit down—really sit down, in the non-gauzy world of our real lives, so that we can stand as a revolutionary voice in this culture.

Twelfth-century Zen Master Hongzhi, in the texts compiled by Monk Puqung, advised that all we need do is:

> ...rest from the remnants of conditioning. Persistently brush up and sharpen this bit of the field. Directly cut through all the overgrown grass. Reach the limit in all directions without defiling even one atom. Spiritual and bright, vast and lustrous, illuminating fully what is before you, directly attain the shining light and clarity that cannot attach to a single defilement.

Overgrown or trampled grass is phenomena. It is every single thing, moment, thought. Where we place ourselves in the grass creates who we are and how we are; it creates what is important to us. When that grass is mown—when that continual self-creation is cut away—what happens? We are complete. The four directions—north, south, east, west—become neighbors; they are all intimate. No one is a stranger; no one is a foreigner. I remember teaching freshman English and receiving a stack of papers written by my students. The papers were awful—shallow, self-serving, fulfilling the requirements of the assignment, but with absolutely no heart or passion. It took such a long night of anger and sadness for me to recognize that the problem wasn't the students. They weren't the "strangers." The problem was that I hadn't learned how to teach them yet. *I* was the "stranger," and I needed to come home to myself, to mow down everything I was putting between us, and begin again.

Hongzhi taught: "Thus it is said that the mind-ground contains every seed and the universal rain makes them all sprout. When that awakening blossoms in the mind-ground, desires fade and the Bodhi's fruit is perfect in itself." Centuries later, the poet William Butler Yeats wrote that one "lifts a flap of paper to discover both the human entrails and the starry heavens." So where will we start?

Han-shan said, "there are birds to help with the sound of singing/but there isn't anyone to ask about the words of the Dharma." What do these words offer our January woes? They don't present an escape: no answer in the book, no one outside to offer comfort. They mean we are home, and guess what? We are sufficient. We are exactly where we need to be to take care of this life. The pen is in our hands; the ink is in our blood, and the world is trembling with possibilities. Or is that just thunder rumbling deep up the mountain where the snow clouds are so improbably huge?

Shitou's Two Sighs

When the monk Tang Ying Feng was about to leave, ancestor Mazu asked him, "Where are you going?"

"To Shitou," he replied.

Mazu cautioned, "Shitou's path is slippery."

Tang answered, "I can take care of myself." He started walking.

When Tang arrived at Master Shitou's temple, he walked around the meditation hall once, banged his staff on the ground, and demanded: "What is the meaning?" Master Shitou said, "Oh heavens! Heavens!"

Tang didn't have a snappy reply to this, so he went back to Mazu's temple to report on his encounter with Shitou. Mazu said, "Go back and see Shitou again. When he said 'Oh heavens! Heavens!' you sigh deeply. Do it twice."

Tang did as he was instructed, and returned to Shitou. He circled the master, banged his staff, and asked the same question as before. But this time Shitou answered by sighing deeply, not once but twice.

Tang was left speechless again. Perplexed, he returned to Mazu and told him what had happened.

Mazu said, "I told you, Shitou's path is slippery."

Practicing the slippery path—like Tang, we get confused, frustrated. Nothing we do accomplishes what we intend. As soon as we get our feet set beneath us, get our bearings and move forward, the landscape changes—we're turned upside down. Winter brings us into this subtle space of spiritual work in varied ways. The path beneath our boots literally gets slippery, with the ground itself hard, offering unreliable support. There is ice hidden beneath compelling beauty. We learn over and over again the value of the attentive step, the caring and careful gesture.

As the winter weather gets challenging, our awareness of discomfort awakens with renewed strength. Our resilience rides the waves of the flu season, the shortness of the daylight, and the sirens' call for more winter sleep. Streets and sidewalks are cold and wet—inadequate beds for the homeless—and the suffering of the most vulnerable is fierce. Time is slippery, less assumed, with something called "a year" ending, and something called "a year" beginning. Mortality and the saccharin danger of the preciousness of a moment passing blow into our bones in winter. Is life passing too quickly? Too slowly? Are we being used well by time? Are we using time well? The slippery path of Zen training is the mind's winter, in all its hidden and sheer ungraspability.

It is in this spirit that we receive a warning from Master Mazu: those who venture from the comfortable, the known, should be awake, he cautions his monk, and in doing so, punches through the glaze of time to alert each of us to the fundamental liquidity of reality. Today the path of Shitou—our path—is icy, and the way of reality excites motion in unexpected directions.

Mazu started the Rinzai and the Yogi schools of Zen, two of the five major schools. He was known as a great "bear" of practice—lumbering and huge, yet always with a contained deftness that could reveal a student's arrogance, like a fish grabbed from a stream's edge and held in the sun. Mazu wintered well. He trained close to one hundred successors for the weather of full-out spiritual life. The eighth century must have been an extraordinary time to study when the two hundred miles between Mazu's temple and Shitou's was a well-worn reciprocal pilgrimage path. The records show them sending students back and forth to be honed and sharpened, even though it is reputed that these two great teachers never met face to face.

Tang was one of these monks, confident and alert, single-minded. But as with each of us, his gifts were also his curse. His tools, though sharp, were used poorly because he was attached to them. Every tool is neutral. It enters into the karmic game of good and bad, of well used and poorly used, when it comes into activity. Molly Ivins, the tremendously irreverent, iconoclastic journalist from Texas, wrote about this in terms of government in her book, *You Got to Dance with Them What Brung You:*

> *Personally, I think government is a tool, like a hammer. You can use a hammer to build or you can use a hammer to destroy; there is nothing intrinsically good or evil about the hammer itself. It is the purpose to which it is put and the skill with which it is used that determine whether the hammer's work is good or bad. If hammers were cussed as often and as vigorously as government, no doubt some Tim McVeigh would have parked a loaded Ryder truck outside a hammer factory by now. Cussing government in a democracy is a peculiar thing to do: it is, after all, us,*

So many of us waste years cussing the hammer, cussing the gifts gone wrong, the spiritual traditions misapprehended, the qualities in ourselves we've used to such ill effects. It is incredibly tempting, and ultimately plain-out stupid.

As Tang was heading out, Mazu asked him the most obvious and difficult of questions, "Where are you going?" It is, in a sense, the perennial question for those who arise from the seat of zazen, of meditation. Now that you have discerned the still point, how will you move and yet not lose the stillness? How will you go forward without leaving home? Where, in the most direct sense, are you going? "To Shitou," Tang replied. Another teacher, another mountain. If Tang has realized that it is not distant, he's yet to make that clear. So, Mazu said, "Shitou's path is slippery." Shitou was a realized teacher so his path was truth. Tang said, "I'll use my own skills to deal with the situation as it presents itself." We may see in this both the reality of a trained adept, someone who will practice unconditionally, who will not be dissuaded, and also the mild arrogance that clouds alertness.

Tang came to Shitou, circumambulated, banged his staff on the ground. Complete, unmediated action. What is outside that? Then he challenged, turning the dharma sword around and pressing the teacher, "What is the meaning?" What does it all come to? What is the raw truth? He was spending himself completely. Shitou simply said, "Heavens! Heavens!" So very much ado about this very moment, such self-conscious drama.

This too was my initial way of engaging formal dharma combat—when a student challenges and a teacher illuminates the Buddhist teachings. There is actually a record of my initial attempt on an embarrassing videotape. My teacher, John Daido Loori, made the mistake of showing a film of monks doing dharma combat at a Zen monastery in Japan. The challenger would shout something really loudly in Japanese. The respondent would shout back with an equal or greater aggressiveness. Invisible exclamation points littered the air, small animals ran for cover. This macho dramafest entered my psyche as the way not to get snagged by the sentimental, to go right to the heart, to just do it! When we had dharma combat at Zen Mountain Monastery, I was the first challenger for the senior monk. I tigered out with my mock Japanese fierce voice, doing my best to do what seemed called for, but I was actually lost beyond lost. For weeks I got variations on, "Jesus, Myotai, what were you so angry about?" Fortunately, the senior was able to deal with my ridiculous mean-guy act, not too differently from Shitou in our koan, "Oh heavens!"

Tang was left speechless and we're left to encounter the teachings of his speechlessness. Shitou's uncontrived response parted the waves of Tang's false confidence. Neither Shitou nor Mazu were known as timid, 'Oh my goodness!' teachers, so this "Oh heavens!" was, in context, a shockingly mild teaching. The moment Tang's expectations were not met, thoughts stopped. Most of us as students do the same thing with face-to-face teaching. We bring the teacher our beautiful understanding and there's a script we're prepared to live out. "I will say so and so and the teacher will go 'Ah!' or 'That's it!' or then the dialogue will head out in this sparkly direction..." My teacher, to my great fortune, would do nothing that I had planned for him to do. The un-puppet, he would catch me unaware that I even had a script, but unable to proceed because it had been thwarted. The intolerable frozenness of those moments was the life I knew needed to be realized and practiced.

The habit of freezing, in anxious speechlessness or in the larger sense of isolating our movement from the movement of the moment, is familiar to most. Less familiar may be the practice of being who we really are, fluid and able to really meet the situation as ourselves. We learn in formal koan study to acknowledge, to let go and begin fresh—that's where the life of the koan is. How does that practice penetrate? We need to acknowledge our commitments to training. Just see them. "I said I would do at least seventeen things with absolute integrity and vigor and I did three, two of them actually with some energy." We acknowledge and then let go. Practicing this way is not artificial or small, not constricted to the formality of training. We hit that open moment when our expectations are crushed and the habit-culture of lifetimes begins rushing in with complaint and hesitancy. Shitou and Mazu worked to help Tang and every student on the slippery path to be free at that moment. A life-breath, theirs is a teaching that goes right into the ice of us, if we inhale right where we are.

To rest as clearly and as dispassionately as we can right where we are is probably, and remarkably, the hardest thing we'll ever do. "If the shit is up to your nostrils," my teacher once said, "it's a good thing to notice that before you start dancing." Then let go of the smoke-being of that reality: the *I am bad...It is bad...I should have done...I could have done....* What is true rest? One of my favorite examples is in the story Martin Luther King tells of a ninety-seven-year-old woman in his congregation, Sister Pollack. She was still working during the bus boycott, walking to her job every day, an old and clearly bent woman. As she was walking one morning, a white man pulled up beside her and begged, "Please, let me give you a ride." She said, "No, it's alright. I'm walking." She kept going. She took fifteen or so steps more, and the man just couldn't stand it. He stopped his car, backed up, and asked her again, "Aren't you tired? Please, let me give you a ride." She looked at him then and locked into his eyes. King quoted her as saying, "Sure, my feet are tired, but my soul is rested," and she kept walking.

King considered Sister Pollack a great inspiration. A year or so later, he went through a time of doubt. He had been in jail six or seven times, and was scheduled to speak at a large meeting one evening. It was the night before his house was bombed, and he had received a series of threatening phone calls. His spiritual drive was weak. He said he went to the meeting and gave his talk but didn't really "sell it." When he finished preaching, Sister Pollack nabbed him and said, "Brother, what is wrong with you? You didn't have much energy." He assured her, "Oh, no, sister, I'm fine." She persisted, "No, you're not; you'd better tell me what's wrong with you. Tell me now." He said, "I'm fine, sister, don't worry." Finally she got him to rest with her in the nature of things, and eyeball to eyeball, she said, "I want you to listen to me. You are not alone. Even if we leave you [speaking of the congregation he was carrying, driving, and inspiring], the Lord is always with you." A few years later she died, but he would often speak of that moment and how it strengthened him over and over again.

Would our rest and our journey be less slippery if we realized as she did that reality never abandons us? If we practiced the truth that is not some other mountain, some other script, some other situation? Tang returned to Mazu, Mazu sent him back to Shitou. Two hundred miles on foot, carrying the words Mazu had scripted for him: "When Shitou says 'Oh heavens! Heavens' you sigh deeply twice." Tang, who was so devoted to freedom, and was finally beginning to get a genuine taste of wonder and doubt, was able to drop his own script, but he immediately picked up someone else's. Even if it was a clear and vital presentation, by the time he delivered it, it had become old news. We should see the living expression of the two sighs and vow to guard that life with every ounce of our energy.

"Where are you going?" the old masters asked from their mountains—solid and massive and sure—asking us to remember wholeness amid our pain and confusion. "Where are you going?" the most vulnerable among us ask, torn and suffering from the distance we've concocted between our vulnerability and that of others, reminding us not to leave their hurt out of our wholeness.

Early in my life I was ripped open by how Martin Luther King asked this of his congregation, and of his own heart. I feel the edge of that so sharply: do I ask myself deeply enough, do I ask my community powerfully enough? Are we alive in the koan of discerning our real work, our unique calling as individuals within Zen practice?

To practice this will involve the commitment to take some chances—to travel on a path known to be slippery. Standing stagnant leads to a frozen heart; moving forward is dangerous in ways we can't imagine. The path of practice takes care of ourselves, our country, our planet; it is a commitment to be

creative, to stimulate the heart of wisdom which can acknowledge the mess we've made without dramatizing it. It can let it
go, and proceed with selfless love. This path will not proceed
by sticking to what is anticipated.

Mazu said, "I told you that Shitou's path is slippery." Our
expectations are limited by our current, meager imaginations
of what is possible. The Way itself is not limited. Why not trust
ourselves? Why not expend ourselves on behalf of the great
Way? To start, we give in to winter's black ice—free to fall, free
to be seen as a fool, free to be wrong. Because when we are at
rest, we can take care of each suffering being. Even when tired,
we walk free, the path always meeting our every step.

Notes and Sources

Hermitage Heart
"Winter Confinement in Shigaraki Village" translated by John Stevens from *Lotus Moon: The Poetry of the Buddhist Nun Rengetsu* (Buffalo, NY: White Pine Press, 1994).

"A Day of Hail" translated by John Stevens from *Lotus Moon: The Poetry of the Buddhist Nun Rengetsu* (Buffalo, NY: White Pine Press, 1994).

"Mountain Retreat in Winter" translated by John Stevens from *Lotus Moon: The Poetry of the Buddhist Nun Rengetsu* (Buffalo, NY: White Pine Press, 1994).

"When the dharma does not fill…" translated and commentary by Robert Aitken from *The Gateless Barrier: The Wu-Men Kuan (Mumonkan)* (Macmillan, 1991).

Sitting in the Dark
The Night Country by Loren Eiseley (Lincoln, NE: University of Nebraska Press, 1997).

"Then I took a lamp…" translated by Susan Murcott from *Women in Praise of the Sacred,* Edited by Jane Hirshfield (New York: HarperCollins, 1995).

Opening the Lotus: A Woman's Guide to Buddhism by Sandy Boucher (Boston: Beacon, 1998).

Touching the Rock: An Experience of Blindness by John M. Hull (New York:Vintage, 1992.

Small Matters
For the Time Being by Annie Dillard (New York:Vintage, 2000).

Threshold
"Poetry" translated by Alastair Reid from *The Essential Neruda*, edited by Mark Eisner (San Francisco: City Lights Books, 2004).

From "Late Prayer" in *The Lives of the Heart* by Jane Hirshfield (New York: Harper Perennial, 1997).

The Ritual Process: Structure and Anti-Structure by Victor Turner (Transaction Publishers, 1995).

Cold Mountain Home
"I like my home well hidden…" from *The View from Cold Mountain,* edited and translated by Arthur Tobias, Jim Hardesty, Jerome P. Seaton, and Jerome Sanford (Buffalo, NY: White Pine Press, 1987).

"…rest from the remnants…" from *Practice Instructions: Dharma Words of Monk Hongzhi Zhengjue of Mount Tiantong in Ming Province*, compiled and with a preface by Monk Puqung (http://www.abuddhistlibrary.com).

Shitou's Two Sighs
You Got to Dance with Them What Brung You by Molly Ivins (New York: Random House, 1998).

Acknowledgements

For many years I was one of the teachers giving talks at a big stone monastery in the Catskills. The instruction for those about to hear a dharma talk is that the words are often "dark to the mind but radiant to the heart." Preparing one is likewise, and depends completely on realizing that whatever you think is going on, that's not it. I learned more from those who heard and read the talks in this volume than they could possibly have ever learned from me. And so my first thanks is to those who have studied with me, and provided that mysterious spaciousness where words and heart, self and other, entangle in radiance.

The doors open into rooms within rooms. The inexpressible gratitude that one must attempt, flailing with quiet joy, for having received what cannot, after all, be given. I stand shaken and stirred by my Zen teachers: Daido Loori; Taizan Maezumi, who made koans live; and Shishin Wick, who placed the heart of the precepts in the heart of the world. And by my poet-mentors, Richard Hauck, who set me looking for the whale; Janet Burroway, who wove all things with sensuous threads; and Jane Hirshfield, who makes me want to become myself every moment.

I also need to thank those who would not rest until what my hermit-soul would quietly hold close, forever propose a greater generosity. That would be, most poignantly, you, Lewis. The early editing of many of these talks was by Rod Huntress, who with deft hand transformed meanderings into whatever meager music one finds here. The great magician Alice Peck, who saw patterns and possibilities, and makes books get born: you are midwife and gift.

Home is one place, and yet. When I return from whatever doubt I've created about it, most often I am called by the love unearned from Rob, husband and best friend. Thank you for asking and asking.

About the Author

Bonnie Myotai Treace, Sensei, is a poet, essayist, and Zen priest, as well as founder of Hermitage Heart Buddhism. She teaches and leads retreats in New York City; Asheville, North Carolina; Gristmill Hermitage in Garrison, New York; and internationally. A lineage holder in the White Plum Asanga, she was the first dharma successor in the Mountains and Rivers Order, and served for over a decade as Vice-Abbot of Zen Mountain Monastery, where she began practicing meditation in 1979. She was the founding teacher and first Abbot of the Zen Center of New York City.

She has published widely in literary and Buddhist periodicals, including *Tricycle, Shambhala Sun,* and *The Mountain Record.* Her writing has also appeared in *The Hidden Lamp: Stories from Twenty-Five Centuries of Awakened Women* and *The Art of Just Sitting: Essential Writings on the Zen Practice of Shikantaza* (Wisdom Publications); *Best Buddhist Writing 2011, Best Buddhist Writing 2004,* and *Buddha's Daughters: Teachings from Women Who Are Shaping Buddhism in the West* (Shambhala); *Water & Its Spiritual Significance* (Fons Vitae Press); and *Lotus Moon: The Poetry of Rengetsu* (White Pine Press).

Myotai lives alongside the Hudson River with one of the world's great English springer spaniels, a cat of indeterminate age, and a man who several years ago made her bride and grandmother in one "swell foop," changing the changing world altogether.

For more information about Myotai Sensei's teachings, please contact:

Hermitage Heart, Inc.
P.O.B. 448
Garrison, NY 10524

Or visit:
www.HermitageHeart.org